21st
Century
Skills Library

COOL MILITARY CAREERS

VIONICS TECHNICIAN

JOSH GREGORY

CHERRY LAKE
Publishing

Published in the United States of America by
Cherry Lake Publishing, Ann Arbor, Michigan
www.cherrylakepublishing.com

Content Adviser
Cynthia Watson, PhD, author of *U.S. National Security*

Credits
Cover and page 1, ©PJF News/Alamy; page 4, ©Everett Collection Inc./Alamy; page 6,
U.S. Navy photo by Mass Communication Specialist 2nd Class Roland A. Franklin/
Released; page 7, DoD photo by the U.S. Air Force/Released; page 9, U.S. Air Force
photo by SSGT Greg L. Davis; page 11, U.S. Navy photo by Mass Communication
Specialist 2nd Class James R. Evans/Released; page 12, U.S. Navy photo by Mass
Communication Specialist 1st Class Christopher Stoltz/Released; page 14, U.S. Army
photo by Pfc. Michael Syner/Released; page 17, DoD photo by Master Sgt. Lance Cheung,
U.S. Air Force/Released; page 18, U.S. Air Force photo by Staff Sgt. Renae Saylock/
Released; page 20, U.S. Marine Corps photo by Lance Cpl. Robert R. Carrasco/Released;
page 23, DoD photo by Petty Officer 3rd Class Shawn J. Stewart, U.S. Navy/Released;
page 24, U.S. Navy photo by Mass Communication Specialist Seaman Adam Randolph/
Released; page 26, U.S. Air Force photo by Senior Airman Nancy Hooks/Released;
page 27, U.S. Air Force photo by Tech. Sgt. Tony R. Tolley/Released; page 29, U.S. Navy
photo by Mass Communication Specialist 3rd Class (SW) Kenneth Abbate/Released

Library of Congress Cataloging-in-Publication Data
Gregory, Josh.
  Avionics technician/by Josh Gregory.
     p. cm.—(Cool military careers) (21st century skills library)
  Includes bibliographical references and index.
  Audience: Grades 4–6.
  ISBN 978-1-61080-445-5 (lib. bdg.) — ISBN 978-1-61080-532-2 (e-book) —
ISBN 978-1-61080-619-0 (pbk.)
  1. United States. Air Force—Aviation electronics technicians. 2. United States.
Navy—Aviation electronics technicians. 3. United States—Armed Forces—Vocational
guidance—Juvenile literature. I. Title.
  UG1423.G74 2012
  358.4'183—dc23   2012001720

Cherry Lake Publishing would like to acknowledge
the work of The Partnership for 21st Century Skills.
Please visit *www.21stcenturyskills.org* for more information.

Printed in the United States of America
Corporate Graphics Inc.
July 2012
CLFA11

RO442956924

TABLE OF CONTENTS

CHAPTER ONE
WHAT ARE AVIONICS? 4

CHAPTER TWO
A DAY ON THE BASE 12

CHAPTER THREE
**BECOMING AN AVIONICS
  TECHNICIAN** 18

CHAPTER FOUR
THE FUTURE OF AVIONICS 24

GLOSSARY 30
FOR MORE INFORMATION 31
INDEX 32
ABOUT THE AUTHOR 32

AVIONICS TECHNICIAN

CHAPTER ONE

WHAT ARE AVIONICS?

Andy looked at each airplane and helicopter carefully as he walked through the gigantic room. His grandfather had brought him to a museum of military

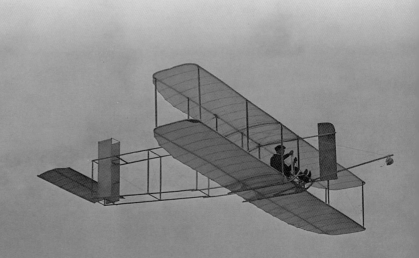

Brothers Orville and Wilbur Wright were the first people to build a powered aircraft.

aircraft. "Look at this," said Andy's grandfather as he pointed at a heavy-looking airplane with a propeller on the nose. "This one was used all the way back in World War II. It was the most advanced plane the United States had back then."

"Really?" asked Andy. "It doesn't look very advanced to me."

"It isn't, compared to newer planes," Andy's grandfather answered. "Airplanes and helicopters can do things now that people could only imagine during World War II. Today's aircraft have all kinds of computer systems and other technology built into them."

"Doesn't that make it hard for pilots to keep track of everything?" Andy asked. "What if that stuff stops working?"

"You're right," said Andy's grandfather. "Those would be problems if pilots had to take care of everything on their own. Luckily, the military has people who make sure those systems stay working the way they are supposed to."

■ ■ ■

Early aircraft, such as **gliders**, were simple machines that were only capable of flying short distances. The earliest motorized airplanes were gliders that had motors attached to them. Eventually, the U.S. Army recognized the advantages of airplanes. The Army began using airplanes in 1909. Since that time, aircraft technology has advanced by leaps and bounds.

Today's military aircraft are equipped with computer-based electronic weapons and communications technology. Other types of technology onboard aircraft protect them from enemy attacks or gather **intelligence**. Even the basic flight control systems of most aircraft are electronically controlled. These electronic systems used on aircraft are called **avionics**.

Avionics systems help aircraft pilots fly in tight formations without colliding.

Today's military aircraft rely on a variety of advanced technologies.

The weapons system on a military aircraft is one of its most important avionic features. Airplanes and helicopters are often equipped with a variety of guns, missiles, and bombs. Sometimes pilots use these weapons to attack enemies. Other times, they are used to protect against incoming attacks. Flying military aircraft is a dangerous job in any situation. It would be even more dangerous if pilots could not count on their weapons to work properly at all times.

LIFE & CAREER SKILLS

Movies, television shows, and video games often show exciting scenes of aircraft, tanks, and ground troops fighting battles. However, they rarely show avionics technicians and other behind-the-scenes military workers on the job. This doesn't mean that these workers are any less important than those who fight in battles. Every member of the military is a necessary part of the organization. Without the hard work of avionics technicians and other workers, the organization would no longer work properly.

Pilots rely on weapons systems to attack enemy targets and defend themselves from enemy aircraft.

Navigation systems are another important feature in modern aircraft. Military pilots often fly in unfamiliar territory where enemies could appear at any moment. The pilots rely on their navigation systems to know where they are going and what is around them. These systems also warn them when other airplanes are near so they don't crash into one another.

Enemy aircraft often have many of the same systems that U.S. military aircraft do. As a result, U.S. aircraft are also equipped with defensive systems to help protect against enemy attacks. Signal jammers can stop enemy **radar** from working and prevent enemy missiles from targeting the aircraft.

Communications systems allow pilots to stay in touch with each other and with commanders and troops on the ground. Being able to communicate is a necessary part of many flight missions.

There are five branches of the U.S. military: the Army, the Navy, the Air Force, the Marine Corps, and the Coast Guard. Each branch uses aircraft to accomplish its goals. Avionics technicians in each branch are in charge of maintaining the various systems. Sometimes technicians even fly on missions to operate the equipment that they are in charge of.

Avionics technicians often refer to manuals to learn about the details of navigation, weapons, or communications systems.

CHAPTER TWO
A DAY ON THE BASE

W hen most people think of military jobs, the first thing that comes to their minds is combat. Almost everyone has seen movies or read books about soldiers

Some avionics technicians work aboard aircraft carriers.

fighting in foreign countries. However, a large number of military personnel rarely see combat. Instead, they work in offices, bases, and other military facilities.

Like other technicians and mechanics in the military, avionics technicians spend most of their time off the battle-field. Avionics technicians work mostly in aircraft hangars on military bases. Many of these bases are located in the United States, but the U.S. military also maintains a presence in other countries around the world. Avionics technicians also work aboard **aircraft carriers** or at temporary military facilities that are set up during wartime.

LIFE & CAREER SKILLS

The U.S. military offers a wide range of benefits to its workers in addition to a paycheck. Military bases provide free housing for employees and their families. Bases also have cafeterias where employees can enjoy free, nutritious meals and fitness facilities to help them stay in shape. Members of the military who live off base receive extra money to help them pay for housing, food, transportation, and clothing. Nonmilitary jobs do not usually provide such benefits to their employees. These are important things to consider if you're thinking of joining the military.

Mornings begin early for the men and women of the U.S. military, whether they work on bases or fight on the front lines. Military facilities usually have wake-up calls sometime between 5:30 a.m. and 7:30 a.m. Like other military personnel, avionics technicians are likely to begin the day with a morning workout and a hearty breakfast.

Much of an avionics technician's job consists of testing avionics systems to make sure they are working properly.

Technicians must make sure that aircraft systems are working and ready to go at any moment.

Technicians use special computer systems to run tests on each of the systems for which they are responsible. Avionics systems are tested before flights so that pilots will not run into any problems on their missions. The systems are also tested after flights to make sure they weren't damaged during the mission. Sometimes a pilot will notice that something is wrong during the flight. When the mission is completed, the pilot lets the technicians know about the problem.

Once a problem has been found, avionics technicians **troubleshoot** the issue. They use their knowledge of electronics and computer systems to carefully examine and test systems until they find the cause of the problem. They make sure everything is wired correctly and check each individual part of the system. They often refer to technical manuals or **schematics** to see what a properly working system should look like.

Once the cause of the problem has been identified, they can begin working on a solution. Sometimes a damaged or malfunctioning part can be fixed using basic tools. Other times, technicians need to install a new system. Once the system has been repaired, technicians make final adjustments so it will work properly.

Some avionics technicians specialize in a certain type of avionics system. For example, Marine Corps aircraft electronic countermeasure systems technicians become experts on the defense systems for a specific aircraft. They maintain the aircraft's defense systems and fly along on missions to operate the systems. Other technicians specialize in weapons systems or a particular aircraft's electrical systems.

Avionics technicians keep careful records of their work. They fill out forms after every inspection, repair, or installation. That way, the military can keep track of each aircraft's repair history.

Military facilities often keep stocks of spare avionics equipment so that it is available whenever needed. Avionics technicians are responsible for keeping track of this equipment so they will know when it's time to request more parts.

Working on aircraft can occasionally be dangerous. Sometimes technicians must climb ladders or use scaffolds to reach parts of the aircraft. Other times, they must squeeze into tight or awkward spaces, or carry heavy tools and parts. They follow safety rules carefully to prevent injuries. Hangars and aircraft carriers can also be very loud places. Technicians use ear protection to help them avoid hearing loss.

Avionics technicians are often under pressure to make sure they get their work done quickly and correctly. Military operations are frequently planned around strict schedules. Technicians must stay calm and avoid making mistakes, even when they are pressured to finish their work quickly. One small mistake could be the difference between life and death for a pilot.

Ear protection is important for anyone working near airplanes.

CHAPTER THREE

BECOMING AN AVIONICS TECHNICIAN

Choosing to join the military is a major decision. Work in the military can be extremely dangerous, even if you work in a noncombat job. Military life often

Important missions often require military personnel to go a long time without seeing their families.

requires you to be away from your friends and family for long periods of time. You also must be willing to travel anywhere in the world at a moment's notice. Once you enlist, you will be required to serve for at least two years after your training is complete. Most people are required to serve longer.

You can't change your mind after you've signed an enlistment contract, so be sure to think carefully before you join any branch of the military. Talk it over with friends and family first. Consider talking to a **recruiter**, as well. Recruiters can answer any questions you might have about life in the military. You can talk to them even if you are unsure about enlisting.

There are a handful of qualifications that all members of the military must meet. First, they need to be in good physical condition. All members of the military are required to stay healthy and exercise regularly. Even though avionics technicians don't often see combat, they still need to stay in good shape to get their work done properly. Willingness to follow orders and work as part of a team are also necessary traits for anyone who wants to join the military.

There are two general categories of military personnel: enlisted personnel and officers. Enlisted personnel are the people who sign up for the military by visiting a recruiter and signing a contract. They usually do not have college degrees. Officers are the leaders of the military. Becoming an officer requires a college degree and strong leadership skills. Avionics technicians are enlisted personnel, but they can become officers by taking classes and working hard after they enlist.

Once you've decided to join the military, you will have to decide which branch is the right one for you. Each branch uses different aircraft and focuses on a different aspect of the military. For example, Army avionics technicians spend most of their time working on helicopters, because the Army rarely uses airplanes. Navy avionics technicians are more likely to work on aircraft carriers, since the Navy focuses on sea warfare. In the Coast Guard, you'll be less likely to travel

Avionics technicians can't be afraid to get their hands dirty.

to foreign countries, because the Coast Guard mainly operates along U.S. coastlines.

Once you have decided which branch you would like to enter, the next step is to visit a recruiter. All branches of the military have recruitment offices throughout the country. Recruiters at these offices take new candidates through the process of enlisting. They begin by giving a test called the Armed Services Vocational Aptitude Battery. It is a multiple-choice test with several sections that cover such topics as math, language, and technical knowledge. The results determine which careers a person is best suited for.

Enlisted personnel in all branches begin their military careers with basic training. Basic training programs last several weeks. During this time, new recruits learn the general skills that all people in the military need. They participate in drills and go through intense physical training. This hard work helps prepare the recruits for the difficulties of serving in the military.

After basic training, potential avionics technicians must go through additional training so they can learn about avionics systems. The exact length of these programs varies from branch to branch, but they usually last for several months. Students spend their time taking classes in electronics and computer systems. They also get hands-on practice with real avionics systems. Once they have completed the training program, they become certified to work as avionics technicians.

LIFE & CAREER SKILLS

Teamwork is a part of everyday life for all military employees, whether they work in offices, on bases, or on the front lines of combat. All members of the military must be able to listen to others, solve problems together, and set aside personal differences in order to accomplish their assigned missions. As a result, people serving in the military often develop close relationships with the men and women they work with. However, they must always be ready to help people they have never met before, too. Try to develop teamwork skills while you're still in school. They'll come in handy in almost any career.

No matter which branch you want to join, you should take plenty of math and science classes in high school to prepare for a career as an avionics technician. You should also take electronics or machine shop classes if your school offers them. Every branch of the military looks for people with knowledge and interest in fixing and building things to fill avionics technician positions.

Knowledge of machines and electronics will make you a good candidate for becoming an avionics technician.

CHAPTER FOUR
THE FUTURE OF AVIONICS

I t's difficult to predict how many military jobs will be available in the future. Throughout most of the U.S. military's history, it was easy to join. There were usually not enough

The military is always looking to recruit skilled, educated people.

people to fill all of the needed positions, so the military accepted most people who wanted to enlist. In the early 2000s, however, a large number of people became interested in military service. The military currently has more people than it needs. There is a waiting list to join. However, this could change at a moment's notice. The military might suddenly need more people if the country went to war.

Those who do find their way into military jobs are paid based on their **rank** and how long they have been serving. Recently enlisted men and women do not earn large salaries, but as they gain experience and move up through the ranks, they can count on regular raises. Yearly pay for enlisted personnel ranges from about $18,000 per year for new recruits at the lowest ranking to about $225,000 for high-ranking officers with more than 18 years of experience.

In addition to base pay, the military offers a variety of bonuses. Some people are given bonuses of as much as $40,000 to join the military. Education bonuses are given to newly enlisted men and women who have completed college courses. The amount of these bonuses varies depending on how many college credits the applicants have earned. Other bonuses are awarded for having special skills, such as being able to speak foreign languages or being able to care for animals.

The U.S. military provides its employees with excellent retirement benefits. Members of the military are eligible for retirement after 20 years of service. Since most people begin their military careers at a young age, they can retire early enough to begin a new career after they leave the military. In addition to the salary they earn in their new jobs, these people receive paychecks from the military as part of their retirement benefits. The military also offers career services to help its retirees find new jobs.

Avionics technicians have many choices when it comes time to find work after leaving the military. The skills they learned

An avionics technician's training provides her with skills that are useful both in and out of the military.

Military service teaches avionics technicians useful organizational and managerial skills.

working on military aircraft might help them succeed at a variety of similar jobs working on **civilian** aircraft. Some avionics technicians go to work for commercial airlines. Others find employment at aircraft manufacturers. There are also positions available for avionics technicians at large companies, government agencies, and other private organizations that own aircraft. Military experience gives avionics technicians an excellent advantage in finding civilian work.

As new technologies are developed, avionics technicians will become increasingly more important. The military will need plenty of bright young people with an interest in electronics. With hard work and dedication, you could be one of them. Do you have what it takes?

21ST CENTURY CONTENT

The Federal Aviation Administration (FAA) is a government organization in charge of regulating flight in the United States. It requires all civilian avionics technicians to become FAA-certified before they can perform maintenance on aircraft. However, FAA certification is not required for technicians who have experience working on avionics in the military. This makes it easier for them to get civilian jobs.

Will you become an avionics technician one day?

GLOSSARY

aircraft (AIR-kraft) vehicles that can fly

aircraft carriers (AIR-kraft KAIR-ee-urz) warships with a large, flat deck where aircraft take off and land

avionics (ay-vee-AH-niks) equipment and electronic systems installed on aircraft

civilian (suh-VIL-yuhn) not part of the armed forces

gliders (GLYE-durz) very light aircraft that are designed to fly without engine power

intelligence (in-TEL-uh-juhnts) information gathered and used by government agencies to plan and make important decisions

navigation (nav-uh-GAY-shun) the science of getting aircraft and other vehicles from place to place by determining position, course, and distance traveled

radar (RAY-dahr) a system planes use to locate objects by reflecting radio waves off them

rank (RANGK) official job level or position

recruiter (ri-KROO-tur) a military employee in charge of signing up new members and providing information to people who are interested in joining the military

schematics (ski-MAT-iks) diagrams showing how a device is constructed

troubleshoot (TRUH-buhl-shoot) to use specialized knowledge to determine the cause of and solution to a problem

FOR MORE INFORMATION

BOOKS

Abramson, Andra Serlin. *Fighter Planes Up Close.* New York: Sterling, 2007.

Meredith, Susan. *How Do Aircraft Fly?* New York: Chelsea Clubhouse, 2010.

Solway, Andrew. *Aircraft.* Chicago: Raintree, 2012.

WEB SITES

Marines—Roles in the Corps: Avionics
www.marines.com/main/winning_battles/roles_in_the_corps/ aviation/avionics
Watch a video about what a Marine Corps avionics technician does.

U.S. Army—Careers & Jobs: Avionic Mechanic
www.goarmy.com/careers-and-jobs/browse-career-and-job-categories/mechanics/avionic-mechanic.html
Find out more about becoming an avionics technician in the U.S. Army.

U.S. Coast Guard—Avionics Electrical Technician
www.uscg.mil/hq/cg1/attc/training/aet.asp#Training
Learn about becoming an avionics technician for the Coast Guard.

INDEX

aircraft, 5–6, 8, 10, 15–16, 20, 28
aircraft carriers, 13, 16, 20
Armed Services Vocational Aptitude Battery, 21

bases, 13, 14, 22
basic training, 21
benefits, 13, 25, 26
branches, 5, 10, 19, 20–21, 22

civilian careers, 28
communications systems, 6, 10

defensive systems, 10, 15–16
demand, 24–25, 28

education, 19, 22, 25
electrical systems, 16

enlisted personnel, 19, 21, 25
enlistment, 19, 21, 25

Federal Aviation Administration (FAA), 28

intelligence, 6

missions, 10, 15, 16, 22

navigation systems, 10

officers, 19, 25

physical fitness, 13, 19, 21
pilots, 8, 10, 15, 16

qualifications, 19

radar, 10
records, 16
recruiters, 19, 21
retirement, 25–26

safety, 16
salaries, 25, 26
schematics, 15
signal jammers, 10
skills, 19, 21, 22, 25, 26
spare equipment, 16

teamwork, 19, 22
tests, 14–15, 21
training, 19, 21
troubleshooting, 15

wake-up calls, 14
weapons systems, 6, 8, 16
workplaces, 12–13, 16, 20–21

ABOUT THE AUTHOR

Josh Gregory edits and writes books for kids. He lives in Chicago, Illinois.